DHARMA RAIN

SAINT JULIAN PRESS

POETRY

OTHER BOOKS BY

TERRY LUCAS

ALTAR CALL
IF THEY HAVE EARS TO HEAR
IN THIS ROOM

Praise for DHARMA RAIN

"Watch your step," warns the speaker in "Vortices," one of the gripping poems in Terry Lucas's *Dharma Rain*. Good advice for approaching Lucas's second full-length collection, for in these poems, "everything enters you." From the grim realities of "The Arrival," "Horse Latitudes," and "A Short History of Baby Incubators" to the wry humor of "Science Fact or Fiction" (about the history of "Giving the finger") and the delicious wit of "Psalm '66" to an amazing series of poems placing John Calvin as a kid growing up in Texas in the '50s, the poems of Lucas's new book confront the mysteries of science, faith, and desire in exquisite forms, delicious language, and keen intelligence.

—Wendy Barker

In these ambitious, far-reaching poems, Terry Lucas alternates between his own spiritual agon, specifically his wrestling with Calvinistic ghosts in the persona of a boy named Calvin, and his eclectic, lyrical investigations of such subjects as wild dogs, the spirit, Tassajara, the New Mexico desert, becoming a poet, survivors of barrel descents over Niagara Falls, and a short history of baby incubators. In his fresh new visions of the world stripped of its former fashions, ideologies, and mythologies, Lucas writes as if he's observing the world for the first time on his own heuristic terms in both dexterously formal and free verse. The result is a bold, often iconoclastic chronicle of a poet who "one day...just left / the stains in the whorls of his fingertips, the taste / on his tongue, and went home forever / to the work that had called him from birth."

—Chard deNiord

DHARMA RAIN

Poems

by

Terry Lucas

SAINT JULIAN PRESS
HOUSTON

Published by

SAINT JULIAN PRESS, INC.

2053 Cortlandt, Suite 200
Houston, Texas 77008

www.saintjulianpress.com

ISBN-13: 978-0-9965231-8-9
ISBN: 0-9965231-8-9
Library of Congress Control Number: 2016948820

COVER ART CREDIT: MAURIZIO SIANI
AUTHOR PHOTO CREDIT: BRIAN BUSCH

CONTENTS

FOR EVERYONE BORN INTO FEAR

DHARMA
RAIN

THE THING ITSELF (A CENTO)

You know how hard it is sometimes just to walk on the
  streets

Downtown, how everything enters you—

Iron straight from the forge, fierce with tiny agitation,

Rain ringing like teeth in the beggar's tin,

Like a sinking ship drowning its lights,

Chalk beds   trilobites   giant ferns

Whirr. The invisible sponsored again by white

Isotopes, pockets, dragonflies, bread:

There is no dictionary for this gathering.

You might think you were Noah

Failing to arrange a taxonomy of allergic substances.

Our lives are like birds' lives, flying around, blown away,

Or some far horn repeating over water—

Do we simply join our arcs

The way a seed is pressed into a hole?

Don't ask me any questions, I've seen how things

Blink-quick, or quicker still,

Tracked under the brown fog of a winter dawn,

Follow the light, the twist and drop of blackbirds from the
  tree.

I.

Everyone's a fugitive. Everyone.

—Spencer Reece

VORTICES

We all eventually stumble into our own story.

Every big bang has an infinite number

Of smaller bangs struggling to get out.

For our purposes there are no other purposes.

Theoretically the atoms in your left hand came from a star

Different from the star that donated the atoms to your right.

Some theories are full of theorists.

And some holes are full of stories.

Black ones with event horizons big enough to hold

All the lines ever written in the universe.

But that's another story.

Watch your step.

THE ARRIVAL

28 December 1895

Two platforms give
Perspective to the opening,

Silent scene from *The Arrival
Of a Train At La Ciotat Station.*

Orthogonals merge, tweezing a
Smoldering dot, growing wheels,

Smokestack, bell—and now the tail
Emerges from the vanishing point, in

Full view of the crowd gathered in the
Grand Café's basement, watching the black

Boiler bulge, fill the screen on the wall with soot
And steam, threatening to burst through studs into

The dining room, break vases of chrysanthemums, plates
Of half-eaten Crepes Flambé—waiters scattering, cutting

Through the flickering, dust-flecked beams of light—never
Shining again with such surprise, such innocence, such living
    black and white.

OVER THE FALLS

Step right up for a ticket to the big event:
too poor, too rich, too proud,
totally disgraced, those whom guilt feeds on
as if they were already carrion,
the Virginia Woolfs who enter their own
imagery, the ones for whom death is a deer park,
a convent, a place in outer space, the impotent,
ugly, acned, lonely, the inadequate opportunists . . .

Annie Taylor in a long black dress
and flowery hat, the first to conquer
Niagara Falls in a barrel. Retired teacher,
looking to make a fortune in tchotchke,
for safety measures sent her cat, Lagara,
the day before to test her Kentucky-oak
drum, held together with seven metal hoops.
Climbing out with her lucky, heart-shaped pillow,
dazed, but unharmed, she said *Nobody ought ever*
do that again. Afterwards she remained
in poverty, posing for pictures, working
as a clairvoyant, and providing magnetic,
therapeutic treatments to local residents.

. . . those who embrace their assassins,
who have felt only the hold of their own
hand, thus to come and go finally
in the same way, with deaths nipping,
small and large . . .

Bobby Leach, circus stuntman,
just appeared one day with his contraption
at the office of the Niagara Gazette,
posing for pictures, announcing his intent
to become the first man ever
to take up the triple challenge:
a trip through the Niagara rapids,
a plunge over Horseshoe Falls,
and a descent by parachute from
the Upper Suspension Bridge
into the river.
                    To his credit
Bobby was successful in predicting
two out of the three daredevil feats.
But how could he have foreseen both
legs shattered, the amputations, gangrene
quickly settling in, his untimely death
years later from slipping on an orange peel?

HORSE LATITUDES

You're driving I-10, somewhere between Las Cruces
and Deming. Feeling grounded. *All Things Considered*
on the radio, stories grazing the brown hills, voices
wet with static, licking at the sparse fence line
of automobile aerials moving west—
something about the legend of The Horse Latitudes,
the roiling vicissitudes of the Cape Horn Ocean
killing the wind, compelling sailors to throw horses
overboard to stay afloat—*They found skeletons, necks
broken, right next to sunken boats.* In the same time frame,
the yellow stripe in the road turns
dark, widens and crosses over into your lane—
a streak of rust, then chestnut for miles. You can see it
beginning to turn again, this time coppery
in smell, and it's damp ahead—definitely
part of your brain says best slow down, says O
God! It's a roan in the road, lying on its side,
tied to the trailer behind a pickup truck,
hindquarters quivering. Quivering
in the blood-soaked arms of two men,
there are children crying, and a woman
is pulling a gun from the cab. As you swing wide,
one if its eyes, an unbroken egg full of white sky,
rolls back and flashes its lightning-red veins.
And in that moment you know everything
in the story is wrong—the ocean, the wind, the killing,
the men, those horses at the bottom of the sea—
they jumped.

SCIENCE FACT OR FICTION

Giving the finger began with warriors
Showing the enemy their bow fingers

As they retreated. Running down the track
From starting blocks of stars, some photons die,

But not before they pass off their batons
Of dim light to neighboring particles

That eventually cross the corneal
Finish line. If only we could see them

Touch the horizon, all stars would blink pink
As they set. Messages are buried deep

In Pi, waiting for ten-digit life forms
To discover them. For millennia,

So many humans have killed, wielding swords
In right hands, brandishing shields in their left,

Hearts have shifted for protection.

OVER THE FALLS AGAIN

. . . too ineffably wicked—all addicts,
Cleopatras, Didos, mystics, faddists,
young sorrowful Werthers, the frigid,
the incurably ill, the made, the phlegmatic
widows who go with the rest of their property,
protestors of this life with emblematic ignitions
and ritual sacrifice, the mourners, the divided
selves, the downright inept and careless . . .

Charles Stephens came from Bristol, England
during the summer of 1920. Father of eleven,
he had a reputation of a daredevil in Europe,
where he'd made a number of high dives
and parachute jumps. On July 11 he went over
the falls in a Russian oak barrel—heavy
with straps for his arms. As ballast, Stephens
strapped an anvil to his feet and took a bottle
of oxygen, in case. When he hit the water
at the base of the falls, the anvil was propelled
through the bottom of the barrel,
taking Stephens with it. The remnants
of the barrel remained trapped until
the iron rings broke away. When recovered,
only the tattooed right arm of Stephens
was still strapped in the harness.
It read *Forget me not Annie . . .*

. . . martyrs, daredevils, the accident
prone, those who cheat "justice"
as Hannibal did, condemned by it
as Seneca was, those who would die
rather than surrender, even en masse
at Masada . . .

Peter DeBernardi built a fifteen thousand
dollar barrel. It was constructed of three
sixteenths of an inch steel plating, twelve feet
long and four and a half feet in diameter,
weighing one thousand five hundred pounds,
and had a keel for direction. In addition,
the barrel had a two-way radio system,
eighteen hours of oxygen supply with a ballast
control, a double hatch assembly,
and a pressurized cabin. It had double
Plexiglas windows so that he could see outside.
When recovered beside the dock by the *Maid of the Mist*,
Peter, who had been drinking, was lifted out
uninjured, wearing only a neck tie
and a pair of cowboy boots.

. . . Step right up, folks, everybody's welcome.

A SHORT HISTORY OF BABY INCUBATORS

All the World Loves a Baby

> —Sign in front of The Baby Incubator
> sideshow at Coney Island, 1941

They began as *child hatcheries* in Berlin
in the nineteenth century, but didn't catch on

until Dr. Martin Couney opened up his clinic
as a Coney Island Amusement Park exhibit.

Parents of preemies, given no hope
from hospitals of their day, gave up

their babies to this carnival attraction—
experimental containers set up in a sideshow

where barkers charged a thin dime
to view a pound or two of barely living flesh

through a pane of glass. Assistants dressed up
in white starched uniforms, posing

as doctors and nurses standing at attention
between cubicles, couldn't prevent the struggling

bodies from dying during an outbreak of diarrhea.
Snuggled between the camels and the elephants,

the bearded lady and the house of mirrors,
nestled in their see-through, straw-lined isolettes,

they passed without mention or funeral,
without gold, frankincense, or myrrh.

SWORDS, SEED, GODS, & GOLD

God came to Abram in heat
of daydream. Said, get thee up

& I will show thee my gash
in the ground, my flowing

River Jordan. Abram woke
his wives, his idols, his pride

of lies, hiding in a cave
named right temporal lobe. Set out

on a journey to the other side
of the fertile scythe with all he owned—

swords, seed, gods & gold—
seeking the wound that heals

not, the chthonic angel in a slot
machine in the middle of a desert

called religion. Then Abram dreamed
that he pulled on God's sweaty handle,

spun his drums until they lined up
as three persons—father, son, & holy

mother. Abram heard a voice
deep in the clatter of God's change

back & forth from one gender
to another. Said, because you bet

on me, you are cursed
with my semen. In your mouth

it will become sermon—a milky
way ever-dying, ever-reborn,

a vision not mine, not yours—
wandering in this desert forever.

WHEN GOD MOVED OUT

At first, He visited the children every weekend:
they'd sleep over in the small chapel
He'd taken on the corner across from
The Divine Hand Palm Reading Parlor.

He bathed them in the baptistery beneath
a mural of olive trees on the banks of the River
Jordan, calling down from His study to stop
splashing while He was answering

evening prayers. Later He'd descend,
tell bedtime stories replete with apocryphal
animal friends, tuck them into sheepskin
pallets He'd made to cushion the whorled-grained pews.

On the Sabbath, of course, God would rest
at the beach in a chaise lounge, call up dolphins
as playmates, periodically check in
with the new girlfriend on His cell phone.

Sundays He'd take them to the movies, slip
into a vacant theater, create something new
on the big screen, or maybe show reruns
of the great flood, the dinosaur extinction.

After the divorce was final, He came around
only once or twice a year—Christmas, Easter—
but He was always there in spirit: the weddings,
christenings, funerals—lurking in the corners
of His children's dreams of eternal punishment.

DARTS

A wooden dart from Stottler's Drug Store
shaped like that famous X-1 Rocket plane,

Glamorous Glennis, could cover childhood
debts: a bag of cat's-eyes lost

playing *for keepsies* during recess,
a switchblade broken playing Stretch

or Mumbleypeg, carbon-steel clinking
against cool rocks lounging beneath August

grass, like the distant sound of front porch
iced tea glasses. Dick Thimig and I

would let darts fly into September
cottonwoods splotched with bulls eyes

after school. Then the weather changed
and I put them away, stared into the dark

eyes of Linda Locklin, went for walks
among unmarked trees, found frozen

patches of grass begging to be flattened,
came home every night, jeans wet and fragrant

with rogue seeds clinging to the first chance
of spreading beyond their provenance. Picture

two coke-bottle-shaped bodies, perfectly lathed
for one another, lying sixty-nine in underwear

drawers, silver nail points sheathed, waiting
for familiar hands to reach in, stroke the treble-

fletching, cradle one in a moist palm, carry it
outside into the heron-still dawn,

arc it through the breathless air
toward the center of a white, paper target.

SUMMER OF '63

Camping halfway up Abajo Mountain,
one ear pressed to my cold air mattress, one
to a Delmonico, six-transistor
radio: fifty thousand watts of sound
—K-O-M-A, Oklahoma City—
Johnny Dark interrupts *the Rhythm*
of the Rain, telling me just what a fool
I've been with the announcement: "Marilyn
found dead in bed at home." At twelve years old,
how could I have known about the pleasure
and the pain born conjoined in the body
Hollywood? Till death do them part. Outside
my bivouac tent, black air huddles closer
to nodding fire, hushes its wheezing voice
as earth's shadow leans against canvas skin
pulled tight across thin ribs with ropes and stakes,
squeezing out the light like white noise filtered
from a song, waves beamed across a nation:
The only girl I cared about has gone
away—along with her she took my heart.

PSALM '66

O, '66 Plymouth Valiant! In you will I put my trust.
Your chromed, Barracuda hood ornament leads me.

Your tuck 'n roll bucket seats comfort me.
Your 400-horsepower Hemi engine will save me

from being shamed by a Biscayne dragging Main Street.
Though I double-clutch down Red Mountain, I will not fear,

for your disc brakes and your Hurst shifter are with me.
Your tubular suspension protects me. Your roll bar

watches over me—a halo of Chrome-Moly black steel.
Your aluminum wheels and posi-traction rear end

will carry me from the Midwest to New Mexico.
Even though I cross-country to San Francisco,

I have no need for a motor hotel. In truck stop
parking lots your double bass exhaust is hushed,

while a waitress prepares a table before me of pork chops,
buttered toast, hash browns, and fried eggs sunny side up.

You anoint my hands with grease. The sweet smell
of gasoline will follow me all the days of my life,

and I will dwell in the pleasures of your back seat forever.

II.

God preordained, for his own glory and the display of His attributes of mercy and justice, a part of the human race, without any merit of their own, to eternal salvation, and another part, in just punishment of their sin, to eternal damnation.

—John Calvin

PROEM

I want every man and woman, every boy and girl in this auditorium to close their eyes and bow their heads because some sinner is quenching The Spirit, some soul is resisting The Almighty Lord by not walking down the aisle in answer to His call. In a moment I am going to pray, and if God is dealing with you—no one looking except for me and The Lord!—just raise your hand and I will include you in my prayer.

Then we're going sing one more stanza of "Just As I Am," and if someone steps out into the aisle, walks down to the front of this holy sanctuary, places their hand in the hand of Jesus, we will sing another verse.

But if no one comes, you will close out this invitation and go out into eternity alone, without God! Do I see a hand? No one is looking except me and the Lord. Do I see a hand? Yes! I see that hand. Is there another? Is there another? I see that hand. Yes! And that one. Is there another? Is there another? Let us pray!

—Altar Call by Evangelist Angel Martinez, 1956

MEET CALVIN

Trained from birth in the most fundamental

tenet of fundamentalism—fear—

Calvin lit the other end of his existential candle

by waxing intellectual—no tear

allowed to drizzle over Sundays of frozen emotion

served up by the biggest Father around,

force-fed by a fanatical mother. Religious conversion?

He faked it!—as well as the claim he'd found

the peace that passeth all understanding.

Later, he lied about the call to preach,

abstinence, celibacy, God's blessings—

but not the adrenaline that forbade sleep,

raised his BP, gave him A-fibs, PVCs,

not about *what hurt him into poetry.*

HE COULDN'T PLAY IN DANCE BAND
BECAUSE DANCING WAS A SIN

But was allowed to take up the trumpet

because it was *The Lord's* instrument

played by angels to call forth plagues and woes

in the book of Revelation. He practiced for hours

each day on his cousin's beat-up Blessing—private lessons

went so well his father bought him a new Conn Constellation.

The next day, after warming up on "Stardust,"

his trumpet teacher told him that he really must

play *the song about a song about love* that night

at the fall concert. After school in the empty band hall,

he closed his eyes and blew through tilted-up bell,

the way he'd seen Maynard do—

he envisioned sinners slow-dancing, a darkening moon,

each note calling down a star from the molten sky.

LOVE LIFTED HIM NOT

He hadn't even known that he was sinking
deep in sin until his mother told him
not to take the grape juice or the wafers
the deacons would pass down the aisle that night—tapers
reflecting on chrome trays—because Jesus hadn't paid
for *his* sins. Eight years old and on his way
to hell because he'd never been so bold
as to walk the aisle for Christ, trust the old
rugged cross. "But God still loves you," said his father.
"And so do we," said his mother.
Next day he heard her talking on the telephone:
"Calvin's under conviction; please pray for his soul."
"Yes," he thought, "I do need help from above,
lest I drown in these angry waves of love."

SURRENDER

Before the final verse of every revival meeting
invitation service Calvin attended as a child,
after the visiting evangelist whipped off
his sharkskin jacket, loosened his Countess Mara
silk tie, God-danced across the podium, lifting up
French cuff-linked wrists to wave the choir silent—

After he slid the sweaty microphone out of its stand,
skipped down the steps, and asked *each man and*
woman, boy and girl in this sanctuary tonight
*to close their eyes, bow their heads…*after praying
for some lost soul to come forward—a sign
to continue the invitation hymn another stanza—

Sister Ila Mae McWhorter's arthritic fingers
would depress the keys on the upper rank
of the Hammond organ to the first chord
of "I Surrender All," Blake's dad would run
down the aisle, sobbing, stumbling, falling
into the preacher's arms. *Not again, not*

Again, Blake would cant, sotto voce,
sinking down into the second row whorled-
grained pew. Then other sinners would come—
or not—either way Pastor Gray would always
introduce Brother Lloyd as if no one knew him,
as if no one had ever known him to surrender
his life to the gospel ministry, to testify

how he was going to put up his store
for sale again, go back to school at S.I.U.,
get his degree in religion, perhaps
even take correspondence classes from Southern
Seminary, prepare himself for preaching
God's word in and out of season—Hallelujah!—
how this time it was real, this time he had
really surrendered to God's will—Calvin would never forget
the way Blake curled up on the pew and lay so still, so still.

LESSONS

1. TMI

When Calvin was ten, his father gave him lessons—
how to please a woman, and how to use his hands
to kill a man—all in the same conversation.
He demonstrated each technique with his index
and middle fingers. The former skill he would not need
for another decade—never the latter. *Too much
information* some might say. But hopping freight trains
in the Great Depression at the same age
was normal for a quarter million children, and his father
was only making sure his son was equipped
with the knowledge he'd had to gain on his own.
Even though Calvin didn't need everything
his father gave him, he was grateful all the same,
and at a young age he became quite the expert.

2. The Old Farmer's Almanac

At a young age he became quite the expert
in *The Old Farmer's Almanac*, reading up
on the days it would rain that fell on the first
of the month. He and Blake would stand outside
Perky's Garage, watch coveralled mechanics
writhe on creepers beneath Fords and Chevys,
while they shivered in front
of the corrugated tin shed, hoping
to be invited in out of the rain.
It worked for the first few times,
then those grease-stained men got wise
to how the boys were working their way to the back,
where the lights were always dim,
waiting for the moment when they could steal.

3. Knowledge

Waiting for the moment when they could steal
a look at the new calendar pin-up—
Betty Grable, Rita Hayworth, Jane Russell—
You boys wouldn't even know what to do
with that—the mechanics laughed—
Now git! And they were right—
but kneeling down in the steaming mud
outside the window for a final view,
unaware that the drizzle they felt would soon turn
into a flood so powerful it would strip
their bodies of innocence, then bathe them
in omniscience—there on virgin knees
on that holy day, the first of the month—
O, how they prayed for that knowledge!

INTERLUDE: WHAT IT WAS LIKE

Calvin got saved when he was eleven—
walked the aisle for Jesus, and Blake asked him
"What was it like?" He was almost seven

and *under conviction.* They were both bent
over their bikes—Blake's Schwinn, Calvin's
Western Flyer—attaching face cards to the frames

with clothespins that frap-frap-frapped when they slapped
against the spokes. "I saw a wall of fire
with no end," he said, "and I heard a voice

calling, *come on over to the other side.*"
Calvin got drafted in nineteen sixty-
seven, walked Vietnamese jungles.

Afterwards, Blake asked him, "What was it like?"
"I saw a wall of fire that didn't end, I saw
faces in the flames, crying *come on in,*

and I joined them." Calvin took shock treatments
at age twenty-seven, strapped to a bed
in Anna, and Blake asked him, "What was it like?"

"I was a wall of fire that didn't end—
I called out with a voice I couldn't hear
over the roar of the faces slapping in the spokes."

4. Systematic Theology

O, how he still prayed for knowledge,
unlike his Systematic Theology classmates.
And even though the readings assigned by Dr. H.
seemed to challenge their faith, they pulled Calvin's brain
toward belief in unbelief—an *Honest to God* starting place
for growing the fruits of the spirit in the ground
of his being: planting lust-seared seeds of love,
serving up joy lightly brushed with envy,
peace scalded in wrath, greed in a reduction
of long-suffering, kindness clarified of pride,
goodness dredged in sloth, and gluttony
glazed with faith—not in more, but less:
roots of fruit intertwined with weeds—
the only kind of heaven he'd seen.

DAY ONE

1. "The Radiant Morn"

The only kind of heaven he'd seen
was between the covers of books Calvin was unpacking
from Del Monte boxes—trying to fit them in
to the narrow shelves behind the desk
on his first day as the Minister of Education,
County Seat, Texas. The intercom squawked
with the church secretary's voice: *Have you seen
Brother Gene?* She was afraid he and Etta Mae had slipped
   away
to the city for lunch like they sometimes did on Fridays,
forgetting all about preaching the funeral already assembled
in the sanctuary. Calvin fumbled around for his Bible,
cinched up his tie, grabbed his graduation suit coat
off the back of the chair, and ran down the hallway.
The organ was already playing "The Radiant Morn Hath
   Passed Away."

2. "Its Glorious Noon How Quickly Passed"

The organ was already playing "The Radiant Morn Hath
  Passed Away,"
when the mother of the deceased (a baby, he later learned,
burned beyond God's reach), pacing beneath the stained-glass
window above the narthex, grabbed Calvin by his gabardine
sleeve and demanded to know *Where is Brother Gene?*
He told her the pastor had been detained,
that he would be conducting the service,
but she would have nothing of it—spitting and screaming
how *her* tithe paid *that preacher's* salary, had built *his* parsonage.
When Calvin stepped behind the pulpit, the family
was seated in the front pew, eyes reflecting chandeliers
like mirrors set deep in the sockets of a pride of feeding lions
angered by midnight hunters flashing their spotlights on
  death.
You may have already guessed the scriptures Calvin read.

3. "The Shadows Of Departing Day"

You may have already guessed the scriptures Calvin read:
the 23rd Psalm, some palliatives from Paul and John—
but you could never imagine how large
the crowd that bled out onto the lawn, nor how small
the closed casket, how little Calvin knew
about its contents—whether whole or in part—
how long the journey from church to cemetery,
the drive home—the long way back, where the west
Texas sun proclaimed the earth flat, and Calvin
doubted all he'd been told about valleys
and shadows and death. The phone call came at 10:00 p.m.—
Brother Gene had just gotten home and heard
the messages on his answering machine. He was sorry,
so sorry, to do this to Calvin on his first day. Calvin agreed.

MAKING UP THE DEAD

He's lost count of exactly how many
embalmed bodies. *It's a job
like any other:* applying the color of life to pallor,
creating an image in the memories of survivors.

Embalmed bodies? It's a job
getting the right pink in the cheeks,
creating an image in the memories of survivors
with red paint, needle and thread.

Getting the right pink in the cheeks,
stitching mouths closed, anchoring the feet
with red paint, needle and thread
so the deceased appear that they are asleep.

Stitching mouths closed, anchoring the feet,
massaging out clots, capping the eyeballs,
so the deceased appear that they are asleep,
are a few of the ways to make up the dead.

Massaging out clots, capping the eyeballs,
applying the color of life to pallor:
a few of the ways to make up the dead—
he's lost count of exactly how many.

IF THE SHOE FITS

The Western Electric black telephone again.
This time from the wife of a deacon who wants him
to see her the next morning. She arrives wearing
Etienne Aigner pumps on her feet
and a husband on her arm. Some sick creep
has been leaving boxes of shoes her size
in their closet. No proof, but they have seen
the deacon chairman staring at her feet
during morning worship, and wonder if
he is the guilty party. Yesterday, turning up
their street, they met him driving away.
Can't you confront him? Didn't you take
counseling classes in seminary that covered this sort of thing?
Besides—didn't you used to sell shoes?

UP YOUR SLEEVE

You pull on the end of a shoe
lace—the aglet—like one of those endless chains of magic
handkerchiefs

and find it's tied
to a dead cow or a shell
cordovan, split-toe, balmoral

wiggling like a worm on a hook,
and you keep pulling on it
because that's all you can do.

And the next thing that comes
is the grass photo-
synthesizing your own yellow sol

into chlorophyll. And by now you're wondering
where it all comes from
but you can't stop—everyone else is watching too,

and like a stew it's all pouring out—
the planets and moons and dust clouds
over Kansas with tornadoes and witches and brooms,

and all the childhood things from your room
come spilling out—your chemistry set
that blew up your desk, and your model rockets

that never got off the ground, your angel
fish named Mary and Joseph
are flopping on the floor,

and you think, *Oh God, no more—*
where is that white dove
that ends this show?

INSIDE THIS HOUSE

Inside this house there is no instant death;
the rheostat is merely turned to dim
as sun and moon dip low but never set.

From the path that leads through forest sedge
windows peel and flicker through the limbs,
but inside this house there is no instant death.

The dream goes on long after one's last breath
is separated from this earthly wind:
sun and moon dip low but never set.

Though shades are drawn to cover gelid flesh,
and those that gather sing their one last hymn,
inside this house there is no instant death.

The verses keep repeating in their heads
as they travel home to kith and kin,
sun and moon dip low but never set.

From this vantage point there's much to dread:
a shadow lies in wait while we all spin
inside this house. There is no instant death.
Sun and moon dip low but never set.

CALVIN'S WORK

1. Shoe Dog

Yes, Calvin used to sell shoes

after rising each morning at 3:00 a.m. to study

existential theologians—Tillich, Buber, Bultmann—

then stepping out into the frozen Texas November
   emptiness,

or the burnt August void—it made no difference

how hot or cold, he had to force the key into his car's

stiff lock, listen to the pistons groan

in the ten-year-old engine he drove to class,

the drone of professors reading their twenty-year-old notes,

the second-hand words of a rabbi who had died not quite

two thousand years before. A fast food fix of mystery

meat and chips on the way to the mall,

and he was ready for the next eight hours—

selling fake alligator shoes to slate-haired women.

2. Preacher Boy

Selling fake alligator shoes to slate-haired women
for seven percent and a fifty-cent spiff for each matching
handbag left him so hungry that during breaks he devoured
Ginsberg, O'Hara, Whalen, Williams—even left
a few smears of his own ink in the margins
beneath the cloud-cloying sky hovering over that parking lot.
Sunday mornings and Wednesday nights, he drove west—
a rural church where he directed music & youth, pretending
to know more about God than teenaged sons and daughters
of farmers and ranchers who knew everything
about how to turn four thousand acres into oats,
wheat, peanuts, sorghum—but nothing about their children
smoking dope, trying to hold on as long as they could
to the ineffable moment captured in their lungs, their groins,
    their half-nakedness.

3. Poet

The ineffable moment captured in their lungs, their groins,
  their half-nakedness

roiled behind the fog-covered windows in that cramped
  curved space inside

the Mustangs and Camaros their parents gave them.

For decades he held onto these jobs, or ones like them

until he quit before he was fired, or was let go

before he quit—sometimes he doesn't remember

anything except the poetry—how the words melted

onto his index finger tracing the lines, how he touched

the bitter elixir to his lips, how blue they appeared

in the mirror washing up before returning to the last hour

of his shift, how one day he just left

the stains in the whorls of his fingertips, the taste

on his tongue, and went home forever

to the work that had called him from birth.

LOOSE VILLANELLE

He once saw poems as Victorian women,
never daring to loosen the strings of their corsets
beneath layers of bloomers and bodices, hidden

from the ordinary, the common, those who were fallen
on hard times or bad love, but wouldn't say "fuck it!"
for fear we wouldn't believe they were beautiful women

(nor if we knew they peed or shat or went to confession
to tell the priest the most carnal obsessions). But it's not
under layers of bloomers and bodices (hidden)

that the vulva of verse will come—it's in the open
grapefruit streets at dawn, gorged with red—not faded pink
poems dressed up like Victorian women—

for Beauty is not the only beauty given—
there's the onset of terror behind the wink,
and the layers of bloomers and bodices hidden

won't stand up to the work of the living
dressed like the dead.
                        So he ripped off those grave clothes
                              he used to believe in—
          exposing flesh
                        and shattered bones—
beside them the bloomers and bodices neatly folded.

III.

What is Reality? An icicle forming in fire.

—Dogen Zenji

DHARMA RAIN

In the summer of 2008 when wildfire descended on Tassajara
Zen Center, the oldest Zen monastery outside Asia, The Forest
Service evacuated all residents. Five monks turned back and
met the fire, saving Tassajara.

—Adapted from *Fire Monks: Zen Mind Meets Wildfire at*
the Gates of Tassajara

It was Dharma Rain
      met you, Dharma Rain
from *granite wine*

      pumped from the creek
through PVC pipe
      soaking wooden buildings,

dirt, stone, skin—
      sprinklers the sound
of sustained violins—

      strings creating their own
sultry atmosphere—
      your fiery, brass choir

waiting for the director's baton
      to cue you in. It was the Fire
Monk Jazz Quintet

      rearranged the score,
re-harmonized the minor-chord flame-song,
      Jump, Jive, An' Wailin'

fire-hose saxophones
        swingin' with your drivin'
hot-rock rhythms

        and log-rollin' bass notes,
    cascading down into the smoke-
        filled Tassajara gulch,

the whole valley smelling
        like the world's original singe—
you, up on the ridge,

        ripping off red blouses
from manzanitas and madrones,
        becoming more aroused

with each naked limb, each torso
        exposed in firelight.
You crowned them one-by-one,

        but couldn't penetrate
the V-shaped ravine, though you tried
        like a groom on his wedding night

but in the end, more out of duty
        than desire, you stumbled drunk
into the bed

        of the garden, soft
glow buried in her
        loam, her mist.

        *   *   *

Conceived of flash
          between earth and sky,
I smoldered three days

          beneath dust. Born hungry
for live oak, sycamore,
          maple—compelled to carve

paths through the chaparral—
          maroon-barked manzanita,
chamise, ceanothus, yucca—

          to enlighten all flesh
in my oven mouth—
          in one breath

to translate a trillion tree lines,
          a billion pages of bay laurel
into fire beetles and whispering bells.

          O Tassajara,
when your lanterns were lit
          along the Engawa

surrounding your zendo
          this morning, I saw you—
 the frost of your skin, your body,

          your vulnerable ground,
fire monk boots making little Buddha-shapes
          in the wet dirt.

I saw your treetops aligned
          like piano keys,
each taut string

          tied to nothingness, waiting
for my vermilion finger
          -nailed touch.

Then I turned
          to the moist commerce
of your temple gate and yurts,

          sheds and chemicals,
pine rooms and cabins,
          birdhouse and pool,

your schist stone Buddha,
          eyes brushed closed,
buried in the bocce ball court,

          calling down my parched tongues
to lap your Dharma Rain, your granite wine,
          to suckle the icicle of you.

SPIRIT

After Campbell McGrath

We construct it from water and motion and breath,
      smoke, tremors, tongues
      of fire, desire to live between
the growing distances of the stars.

It is, for all its freedom and aspiration,
      an artifact of human agency—
      the universe become conscious,
poured into cracked urns of flesh.

Its insistent voice mirrored by a hungry ear,
      like the lesser light that rules the night
      reflecting the ancient of days. Old
as the odor of resin-soaked wood on the pyre,

dancing to blood-orange flames,
      fashioned from the atmosphere,
      dark matter, energy, air,
shaped and assembled deed by deed,

and finished with feathers of ice.
      We build it on a loom that turns
      straw thoughts into golden bullion,
then lock it in its chest and hope it can save us.

RECYCLING

I am wheeling the recycling bin
down the driveway, the steep
pot-holed driveway, eighteen percent
grade, making it impossible
for trucks to negotiate
up through freighted foliage to our house.
I am thinking about the plastic Arrowhead
water bottles, the broken down
cardboard boxes, the Ball Mason jars
with a faint grape odor
I am sending out into the world
after having consumed their contents—
I am wondering where they will go,
if I will see them again, and if I would
recognize them in an altered form
or universe.
        I am wondering about the day
the wood pulp in the cardboard was conceived
from a single photon of sunlight striking
one green leaf of perhaps the great-
great-grandmother of this eucalyptus tree
or that balsam fir. And I am amazed at the thought
of breathing in molecules of air,
exhaled from plants, as well as from people
dead for years: Darwin, Shakespeare,
Whitman, Crane swirling in my lungs—
their embered words, unreadable
heat signatures, along with the last breath
sucked from the chest of some rapist
on death row, a thief
hanging on a cross by nails

fashioned from iron smelted in a star
gone nova over five billion years ago—
the same metal hammering through my veins,
feverishly trying to get more
oxygen to my legs, as I walk
back up the crumbling asphalt,
loose gravel anting toward the ocean—mother
ocean stretching up as tall as she can with every wave
for a glimpse of her prodigal children returning home.

IN THE SHAPE OF A WOMAN

For Janet

I've loved many women,
But there is only one
In whose arms I've felt
At home, her arms transformed
Into the frame of the house
Where I was born,
In which I secretly worried
A small opening in the bare sheetrock
Of the closet behind winter
Coats and rain gear pushed back
Into the far corner, the hole growing
Each time I hid from the shouting
That nightly flowed like lava from underneath my parents'
Bedroom door, so by the time it all erupted,
Spewing my father down the hallway
Then out of the house for good,
I had created a space between the walls
Where I fit in between two of the fragrant
Studs that were warmed by the furnace
As the air rose from the basement
Through the metal ducts strapped to them.
This is not about how my parents divorced,
For they didn't, nor is it about my parents
At all. This is about coming home
For the first time, when you had no idea that home existed
In the shape of a woman, when you didn't know
She was already digging through the other side
Of your closet wall to get to your secret
Place, and how she helped you,
And how you helped her
Pull you through completely.

NEW MEXICO SIGHTING

Melanistic Canis Latrans

At first we thought you a wild dog, at least partly
fed by Navajos—your erect body, shining
like a seal's, soaked with the afternoon
sun, was all we could make of your gaze
at two hundred yards. But when you turned
and loped into the desert, silhouetting your muzzle, your tail
swaying like a juniper bush, as much at home among the sage
as sage itself, we knew that you were not
headed to hogans on the horizon. Continuing our descent
down the plutonic spine that percolated through
this plateau twenty-six million years ago, we lost
sight of you, but still whispered as if you were the trickster
god we didn't want to wake, a dream we didn't want
to leave, longing for another glimpse, somehow
to confirm your presence, your mystery—and ours.

TAOS PUEBLO

The bell tower of Saint Jerome is still
standing
over mortar, straw and brick
still burying
her red willow dead without
caskets
the Spanish brought.

Only wooden crosses
with Christian surnames
above the mica clay
remain.
Tewa names below
their swollen tongues
that day—huddled around the story
teller, while mother Mary rained
fire and brimstone from her black cannon—
even now only written down
on zephyr's breath.

The bell tower of Saint Jerome is still
ringing
its hands of clay
still cracking and bleeding
for no one
will dress them
but the sun.

The masses
still kneeling not far away,
the blue lake ribbon
with its red willows—
safe.

The stream knows its banks
need not turn
no matter how much rain
or snow or hail—
mother earth embraces all the children
sitting in her lap
but only whispers stories
to her own.

SHIPROCK

Tsé Bit 'a'i

Cutting your way through dust storms, waves
Of sand blow over your prow, settle on foils of stone,
Wash down the ribs of your hull to crystal sea.

> *The Navajos say you sailed from the north,*
> *A great bird saving their people from the flood,*
> *Crashing into the desert, burying all*
> *But your wings and tail: sole cremains of salvation.*

What is it that makes a man or woman
Set out on foot for you? Your jagged masts that reach
For gibbous moon? Ancient lens of atmosphere?

> *The old ones still believe the blood*
> *Will return to petrified feathers,*
> *Carry them away when the flood returns.*

Grasses and sedges with no names, abandoned
Frames of cars and trucks, a valley of dried bones
That will never rest, that will never rise again?

> *Shiprock! Cry out from beneath the desert;*
> *Call your brothers and sisters from the flood.*

The overwhelming flood of sand
Is all that will mark their graves.

> *Sand enough to stem the flood.*

SONG

They walk on the fur of the earth,
Buzzed close to spires of cool basalt

Temples that honor ancestor rock,
No longer bleeding hot from virgin veins,

Flooding the forest's floor, drowning all
In its roar: a holy Sabbath without

Celebration, hairs of midnight ocean
Fog wrapping around scabrous thighs.

The earth rises like a pillow fluffed
At the edge of the sea, night's open wound

In the body of ice reclining on the continent
Covered with a poultice of mica-schist, backlit

With moon's black light. A flashing of life—
Diaspora, riding the comet spawn, arcing the sky

Reaching for the southern surface.

MAKING ANGELS, BUILDING GRAVES

Farmington, New Mexico, 1959

All afternoon snow fell on the graves, leveling the fresh
      sunken ones, completely
Burying smaller pillow-sized headstones,

Leaving only the tallest monuments as frozen waves,
      wrapped in granite shadows. Through the elms,

A building that resembles a church—is that a steeple or a silo
      that shines under gazes of the faithful

Decay of light exchanging photons for chokecherry flesh?

*   *   *

When they bladed out Knollcrest Drive, Apache teardrops
were broken loose from their pearlite beds: translucent,
obsidian spheres that migrated to roadside rock shops, slept
in wooden bins beneath hand-painted signs: *Feldspar,
Hornblende, Biotite, Quartz.* Some were gathered into garages
of ten-year-old collectors, displayed in a science fair project:
"Further Proof of Volcanism in the Four Corners Area of
New Mexico." Beckland Hills edition was built atop a burial
ground without a nod to the metamorphic myths: Great
Father, Big Pacacho—their bleached bones wedged in
crevices on the faces of cliffs. Whoever owns an Apache
teardrop will never have to cry again.

*   *   *

We are circinate: a trudging ring of carded woolen overcoats,
    scarves and hats. A living crop
Circle, trampling snow from black limousines to gravesides,
    trails of ants carrying downed moths, praying

Mantises, ninos de las tierras. Lowering the bodies of our
    mothers, our fathers, we see the intricate lace
Connections between snow crystals, their deliquescence,
    falling stars, ligature trailing,

Lying in perfect isolation on the frozen surface.

We flap our arms and legs in the snow,
    making angels or building graves, depending
Upon how you look at negative space—
    flying or dying in granite shadows.

THE WATCHMAKER DREAMS

of moving gears and numbers,
hands on clocks that once hung in his shop—not hands but
   arms,

the shorter ones hovering
over the hour of his death twice a day, longer ones

waving past the minutes, lying along the berm
of the curve like victims, some

accident, like a necklace of platinum planets
in transit across the sun—

a string of black pearls in time-
lapse, a repeating Earth. How many nights had acorns

pummeled the roof, the redwood
shingles echoing through the forest like two rim shots

on a snare, the hollow sound
drawing him out of his sheath of sleep, dragging his bent

silhouette to the other
side of the bedroom, where he embraced the windowsill

like a tired lover, watching
the moonlit leaves fold into shadows. How many nights

had fluorescent hands passed through
the darkness captured beneath the face of his bedroom

clock—tonight, only ciphers
offer up their blinking crimson prayers, imploring him

not to forget the numbers,
not to forget the numbers.

INFINITY

If infinity
really exists,

that tiny package
the big bang came in

contains more than everything—
precisely one more present than the last,

and then one more forever, all wrapped in ribbons
of Mobius strips. If infinity really exists, every day turns out

to be lightning's birthday. Each flash of every blown-out
   second,
a train emerges from inside a twisted tunnel, where the tracks

have crossed without derailing cars, carrying passengers
dressed in coats and hats like ours, staring at our faces

in the windows, not a single hair on their heads
uncloned, each unbrushed thought falling

wildly into place, each whorled
fingertip on each cold,

pane of glass—
a kiss.

RETURN OF THE PURPLE MARTINS

Wichita Falls, TX, 1985

A million feathers preen the evening sky, comb out
the yellow, gold and red strands, until black
is a word for world, a tornadic pulsing
thread, spooling back to the first
nest of twigs as thin as tears
or thoughts lost in the
hollow-boned dance
arcing toward the
eye of the elm
until the final
purple martin
spirals
in.
Until
the first
purple martin
spirals out of the
eye of the elm, arcing
toward the hollow-boned
dance, lost in the thought of
tears as thin as twigs, spooling
forward to the next nest, a tornadic
pulsing of yellow, gold and red threads
until blue is a word for world, combing out
a million black feathers preening the morning sky.

TO THE FOG

And then you wake up one morning to the fog
surrounding your house like a heaven,
like the first time you drank a whole bottle
of white wine alone. You get dressed for your walk
down the path that you walk on each day.
You look to the horizon, the shouting
sun now more like moon's soft song. One muted tone
behind sky's veil. You notice the lichen-
covered stones greeting each step, the geometry
of downed limbs scratching at low tide,
the snowy egret you surprise, plumed head
turned on its side, sweeping the mudflats, improvising
a way to catch breakfast in suffused light—
all of this and more, normally hidden in plain sight.
But an orchestra's warming up behind the curtain:
commuters leaning on shrill horns, distant
sirens rising, the engines of this world
revving up their clear intent to perform
something short of a miracle. O fog
of morning, hover in the hollows of this day,
remain in its low places, to rise up again
when we need not more, but less.

ACKNOWLEDGMENTS

I am grateful to the following magazines, journals, and presses in which some of these poems first appeared, sometimes in different versions and with different titles:

200 New Mexico Poems: "Shiprock"

Buffalo Carp: "The Arrival" and "Swords, Seed, Gods, & Gold"

Clementine Unbound: "Psalm '66"

The Comstock Review: "Making Up the Dead"

Diesel (The Anthology of the San Gabriel Valley Literary Festival): "Darts," "Interlude: What It Was Like," "Proem: Altar Call," "Summer of '63" and "Surrender"

Fifth Wednesday Journal: "Dharma Rain"

The Harwood Review: "Taos Pueblo"

From East to West Anthology: "Song" and "Taos Pueblo"

Marin Poetry Center Anthology: "Lessons: 2. The Old Farmer's Almanac," "3. Knowledge," and "Recycling"

MiPOesias: "Horse Latitudes" and "When God Moved Out"

New Mexico Poetry Review: "Making Angels, Building Graves"

OVS: "The Watchmaker Dreams"

PoetsArtists Magazine: "Return Of the Purple Martins" and "The Thing Itself"

Ricochet Review: "Spirit"

Solo: "Up Your Sleeve"

Southeast Missouri State University Press: "New Mexico Sighting"

My thanks goes out to all of the poets from whom the lines to "The Thing Itself" were taken. Their collective body of work, not just the poems listed in the "Notes" section, has called to me and enabled me to become a better poet.

Thank you Suzanne Buffam for your insightful edits to my earliest draft of "The Thing Itself."

Thank you to Chard deNiord and Jacqueline Gens for accepting me into the New England College MFA program, and for your support and encouragement during and after graduation.

Thank you to my dear friends and colleagues at Trio House Press, Tayve Neese and Dorinda Wegener, who have given me invaluable advice about many of these poems while they were fresh on the page, as well as about the ordering of the sections and some of the poems in this book.

Thank you to my friend and poet, Jim Benton, who is always there for me when I need straight talk and honest feedback.

Thank you, Michael Waters. Your voice is always in my ear, and your influence is always evidenced in my work, even in poems you've never seen.

An incalculable debt of gratitude goes to the late Keith Wilson, my first poetry professor at New Mexico State University who, in 1970, inspired me with his own work and encouraged me, as only he could, to begin writing apprentice poems, including "Shiprock," a poem that not only took decades to complete, but that developed into the sequence of New Mexico poems that appears in this book.

Finally, my deepest gratitude goes to Janet, who has made it possible for me to devote my full attention to the work that has been calling to me from birth, and who has been there with her support, and with her discerning ear and eye for a decade, so that I might be the best writer I can be.

NOTES

"The Thing Itself"

This poem is a cento. Each line, including the title, is
borrowed from a different poem:

The Thing Itself is taken from the title of the poem
"Not Ideas About The Thing But The Thing Itself"
by Wallace Stevens.

*You know how hard it is sometimes just to walk on the streets
/ Downtown, how everything enters you* is line 1 from
"Quantum," written by Kim Addonizio, published in
Tell Me, BOA Editions, Ltd.: Rochester, 2000.

Iron straight from the forge, fierce with tiny agitation is line 1
from "Life Near 310 Kelvin," written by Greg Keith,
published in *Life near 310 Kelvin*, SLG Books:
Berkeley, Hong Kong, 1998.

Rain ringing like teeth in the beggar's tin is line 7 from
"The City In Which I Love You," written by Li-
Young Lee, published in *The City in Which I Love You*,
BOA Editions, Ltd.: Brockport, New York, 1990.

Like a sinking ship drowning its lights is line 57 from
Altazor, "Canto I, excerpt," written by Vincente
Huidobro, published in *Poems for the Millennium, Vol. I*,
University of California Press: London, 1995.

Chalk beds   trilobites   giant ferns is line 4 from "The
Fetus' Curious Monologue," written by Amy Gerstler,
published in *Ghost Girl*, Penguin Books: London,
2004.

Whirr. The invisible sponsored again by white is line 1 from "In The Hotel," written by Jorie Graham, published in *The Best American Poetry 1994*, Simon & Schuster: New York, 1994.

Isotopes, pockets, dragonflies, bread is lines 5 from "Crycek: The Confessions," written by Susan Wheeler, published in *The American Poetry Review, Vol. 28/No. 2*: March/April 1999.

There is no Dictionary for this gathering is line 93 from "Draft 55: Quiptych," written by Rachelle Blau DuPlessis, published in *The Best American Poetry 2004*, Scribner: New York, 2004.

You might think you were Noah is line 23 from "Nazareth By Rail," written by Matthew Niblock, published in *Scream When You Burn*, Incommunicado Press: San Diego, 1998.

Failing to arrange a taxonomy of allergic substances is line 21 from "Flower," written by Chris Gordon, published in *Scream When You Burn*, Incommunicado Press: San Diego, 1998.

Our lives are like birds' lives, flying around blown away is line 31 from "Drone and Ostinato," written by Charles Wright, published in *Negative Blue*, Farrar, Straus and Giroux: New York, 2000.

Or some far horn repeating over water is line 9 from "Nostalgia of the Lakefronts," written by Donald Justice, published in *The Best of the Best American Poetry*, Scribner: New York, 1998.

Do we simply join our arcs is from line 55 from "Midway," written by Gabriel Spera, published in *The*

Standing Wave, Perennial (HarperCollins): New York, 2003.

The way a seed is pressed into a hole is line 11 from "Prayer," written by Kim Addonizio, published in *Tell Me*, BOA Editions, Ltd.: Rochester, 2000.

Don't ask me any questions, I've seen how things is line 18 from "1910 (Intermezzo)," written by Frederico Garcia Lorca, published in *Poet in New York*, Noonday Press: New York, 1994.

Blink-quick or quicker still is from line 2 of "Thinking," written by Matt Rader, published in *Grain Magazine, Vol. 31, No. 2*: Saskatchewan, 2003.

Under the brown fog of a winter dawn is line 61 of "The Waste Land," *I. The Burial of the Dead*, written by T.S. Elliot.

Follow the light, the twist and drop of blackbirds from the tree is line 9 from "So Here by my Harangue to God," written by Jim Nason, published by *Grain Magazine, Vol. 30, No. 3*: Saskatchewan, 2003.

"Over the Falls" and "Over the Falls Again"

The italicized lines are either direct quotes or reworked passages from William H. Gass's *The World Within the Word*, Basic Books: New York, 1978.

The narratives of the daredevils who went over Niagara Falls are taken from various Wikipedia Articles.

"Meet Calvin"

> *The peace that passeth all understanding* is from the New
> Testament letter by Saint Paul to the Philippians
> found in chapter 4, verse 7: *And the peace of God, which
> passeth all understanding, shall keep your hearts and minds
> through Christ Jesus.*
>
> The abbreviations "BP," "A-fibs," and "PVCs" refer
> to blood pressure, atrial fibrillations, and pre-
> ventricular contractions.
>
> *What hurt him into poetry* is from W.H. Auden's poem,
> "In Memory of W.B. Yeats,": *Mad Ireland hurt you into
> poetry.*

"He Couldn't Play In Dance Band Because Dancing Was a
    Sin"

> "Blessing" refers to the E.K. Blessing Company of
> Saint Louis, MO, that has made trumpets since 1906.
>
> *The song about a song about love* refers to "Stardust," the
> first major song ever written about a song that didn't
> exist, composed by Hoagie Carmichael in 1927.
>
> "Maynard" refers to Maynard Ferguson, the Canadian
> jazz musician and bandleader who had the habit of
> lifting the bell of his trumpet above horizontal as he
> played.

"Love Lifted Him Not!"

> The title is taken from the Hymn "Love Lifted Me"
> containing the first stanza lyrics: *I was sinking deep in
> sin, far from the peaceful shore, / very deeply stained within,*

sinking to rise no more / Then the master of the sea heard my despairing cry, / from the waters lifted me, now safe am I.

"Lessons: 4. Systematic Theology"

Honest to God is the title of a controversial book written in 1963 by the Anglican Bishop of Woolrich, John A.T. Robinson, that criticizes traditional Christian theology.

"Day One"

The titles of all three sections of this poem are taken from lines of the 1864 hymn, *The Radiant Morn*, written by Godfrey Thring.

"Dharma Rain"

Dharma Rain was the nickname given by the monks at Tassajara Zen Center to the sprinkler system they fashioned from PVC pipe that carries water from the creek to the roofs of the main buildings to keep them damp when threatened by wild fires. When the system ran for the several weeks prior to the confluence of wild fires that threatened Tassajara in the summer of 2008, it created its own climate in the valley that helped to deplete the fire of its energy as it descended upon the grounds of the monastery.

ABOUT THE AUTHOR

Terry Lucas is the author of two award-winning poetry chapbooks (*Altar Call* and *If They Have Ears to Hear*), and the full-length poetry collection, *In This Room* (CW Books, 2016). His work has received numerous awards, including the 2014 *Crab Orchard Review* Feature Award in Poetry, the fifth annual Littoral Press Poetry Prize, and five Pushcart Prize nominations. Terry's poems, reviews, and essays have appeared in dozens of literary journals, and he has taught in the Chicago Public School System as a Master Poet in the Von Steuben Metropolitan Science Center's Writing Center. He is a 2008 poetry MFA graduate of New England College, and currently the Co-Executive Editor of Trio House Press, as well as a freelance poetry coach.

More about Terry and his work can be found at www.terrylucas.com.